Be Successful By...

Learn to Save By Going to Investment School for Beginners

Find Your Guidelines to Create a Stock Portfolio **By Neil Caine**

Contents

Preface

The information about investments or making sound investment decisions is full of contradictions. Everyone wants to invest in the stock market in hopes of becoming rich overnight. However, it takes more than just investing your capital into stocks. There are many different investment strategies and each investor subscribes to a different one at different times. One single strategy doesn't work for all. This book entails detailed information about the workings of a stock market and steps to make sound investment decisions. The last chapter of the book explains various benefits of attending an investment school and how it can help the reader gain extensive knowledge about the market.

The Importance of Investment

Money plays a vital role in everybody's life. Building a decent amount of wealth is crucial in today's world. Some people have so much money they won't be able to utilize all of it in a single life span, whereas others are struggling to scrape up enough to eat three times a day. So, investment is important to ensure you live a comfortable life. Everyone is capable of setting some amount of money to the side for the rainy days. However, you need to note that savings and investments are two different things. When you invest money, the amount grows. You get a return, and the money keeps flowing in. The reason why rich people keep getting richer is that they invest. The money they invest increases because they earn an ample amount of interest. Then, they use a bit of money to buy assets and invest the rest. It is a cycle that ensures a steady flow of income. People keep injecting money into different ventures.

Here are a few excellent reasons why investment is important for everyone.

Inflation

Saving an enormous amount of money is not necessarily a bad thing. However, having your money sit under your mattress or in the closet is not a good idea. It is risky because you never know when someone might break into your house. If a criminal suspects or seesa large amount of cash, they will attempt to rob you. No one wants to put their families in such a risky situation. That's why many people keep their money in the bank.

There is no doubt that the returns aren't very high. However, keeping the money with you and not rotating it or investing it is bad for the economy. If everyone starts going down the same path of saving money in their closets, it will create a shortage of money. In simple economic terms, there will be scarcity. The demand for a product increases when it becomes more scarce. A product's price also rises with its demand. The price of money being high is an increase in inflation. Inflation in small amounts is tolerable. However, if it goes over a certain amount, it can negatively impact the economy as well as the people.

Retirement Savings

This one is a no-brainer. Thousands of people invest their money or keep them in the bank in their retirement accounts. Overtime, they earn a good chunk of interest, providing them a financial cushion when they get older. It is recommended you invest some money when you are young and earning a sufficient salarywhile also being able to manage your expenses. Some private organizations don't support pensions for their employees. In that case, it is especially crucial for you to invest.

Investing in retirement savings also acts as a financial safe haven for your family. A retirement plan is helpful because you wouldn't have to be a burden for your children. Depending on your children in your old agewon't bepleasant.

Spend and Save Wisely

Allowing all your hard-earned money to sit in the safe is pointless. When it comes to your money, you should spend some, save some, and invest some. Let your cash see the light of the day. The minute you give your money the right direction to follow, i.e., investment, it will come back to you tenfold. If it wasn't already clear enough, your money could earn more money for you. Focus your investments on plans that work with your future. If you don't have much knowledge about financial investment, then study or hire a financial advisor.

Real Estate

Most people are aware of investing their wealth into savings or retirement accounts. However, if you have a business, it could be especially crucial for you to invest in making your business grow. When entrepreneurs put their money into sound investments, they grow their profits and income year after. Doing so brings stability to your life and gives you peace of mind. It ensures that you have some form of steady income you can rely on if things don't work out. With several corporations going into bankruptcy, investing is undoubtedly a smart business decision to make.

Most people tend to make traditional investments, such as investing in real estate and stock, while others invest in non-conventional methods, such as bitcoin mining.

These methods help businesses and individuals boost their investment portfolio, enabling them to invest in better places.

For hundreds of years, real estate has been a sound investment method. It is a good option for individuals and businesses alike. The best part about investing in real estate is that it rarely crashes. If you want to secure your money, invest in real estate, especially commercial real estate. Buying commercial properties and renting them is an age-old practice that results in a steady flow of income.

Conduct thorough research to explore all your options and then buy a property that will generate the most income and be feasible years after your purchase.

The reason why investing in real estate is profitable because through rent, most of your personal expenses are covered, and you will have left over income that you can further invest in other places.

Stocks and mutual funds are also a form of increasing your wealth. Most people buy stocks and see a hefty return in terms of profit.

People tend to invest in different stocks to diversify. Don't put all your eggs in one basket, and invest in a variety of companies in different industries, such as tech, precious metals, oil, and so on. You will increase your chances of success, no matter the economic conditions.

Investing in bitcoin mining offers huge profit-making potential. You can acquire bitcoins without having to worry about software, bandwidth, and electricity, and so on. However, before investing in bitcoins, do extensive research, and proceed with caution. Learn how bitcoin mining is done, and invest at your own pace and comfort.

Workings of a Stock Market

The stock market is a place where sellers and buyers connect to purchase and sell stock investments. Stocks are usually bought online when you have enough funds. You can buy stocks by opening a brokerage account, employee retirement plan, or via robo-advisor.

To invest in the stock market, you don't have to become an investor. Anyone can buy stocks. As soon as you purchase your first stock, you will be enlisted in the list of investors from around the world. People buy stocks to increase their wealth over time. Remember, it is not quick money. Also, before investing in a stock market, study the market, find out how it works, come up with a few introductory investments, and then buy stock.

How does the stock market work?

The concept behind the workings of a stock market is fairly simple. It works similar to an auction house. The market enables sellers and buyers to make trades and negotiate stock prices. The market works via a network of exchanges. For instance, in New York Stock Exchange, companies list their shares through a process known as initial public offering or IPO. The investors buy those shares allowing the company to raise wealth so it can grow. Investors can also sell and buy shares amongst themselves. The exchange keeps track of all the transactions and the demand and supply of the stocks.

The very first stock market was founded in Europe in the 16th and 17th century by the Dutch East India Company. The Dutch East India Company employed a hundred ships to trade gold and other items, such as porcelain and spices, around the world. Eventually, they experienced a shortage of money for their next expedition. To raise funds, they asked the citizens to give them some money in exchange for profits brought by the ships. Savvy investors of the time invested their money. The shares were sold in coffee houses and shipping ports. Investors enabled the company to send ships to even more voyages increasing profits for both themselves and the investors.

Stock markets started in the US in the late 18th century. The very first stock exchange was the Philadelphia Stock Exchange. It was founded in 1792.

The prices of shares in the stock market are set in various ways. As mentioned earlier, the most common method is through an auction process. The bid price is the price someone is willing to buy the stock at, and the offer price is the price someone is willing to sell at. When the bid and ask or offer price coincides, that is when a trade is made.

There are millions of traders and investors who buy and sell at different prices. Each stock has a different value, and each day the value changes depending on how the company is doing. If the company is doing well and making plenty of profit, the price of the share will go up or remain steady. However, if the company is not making enough profit, it will slowly lose investors. This is where the demand and supply curve comes in. As the investors lose interest in the company, they don't want to buy the stocks. The lack of demand reduces the share prices, which ultimately reduces the company's market value. The only way it can increase its share price is if it starts making a profit again.

A stock exchange is a convenient platform for people to conduct trade. Some people use stockbrokers to help them make a trade. Stockbrokers are the middlemen between the buyers and sellers.

Some stock markets make use of professional traders to help them maintain bids and offers. Sometimes, the seller and buyer may not find each other. The professional traders are known as market makers or specialists.

Benefits of Stock Market

Every business owner wants their company to be listed in the stock market because of the many benefits.

- Listing your company in a stock exchange means the shares are ready to be liquidated by the shareholders any time they want. All they need to do is sell the shares.
- It helps companies raise funds to grow profitability. They issue more shares in the market for more funds.
- When a company's shares are publicly traded, it attracts potential buyers as well as talented employees. A company doing well in the stock exchange is sought after. Investors want to invest, and employees want to work there.
- Having greater visibility via a stock exchange is advantageous to the company because it results in the share prices going up.

- Shares listed in the stock market can be used as currency.

Reasons for Buying Stock

Buying stocks help an individual grow their wealth. In the long run, the benefit of investing in stock outweighs holding money in cash as savings. Trading different stocks helps individuals spread their risk across a variety of economic sectors, asset classes, geographical locations, and so on. Your money isn't tied down in one place. If one company isn't doing well, you have others to lean on.

Some stocks are a source of regular income for many people. In some cases, even if the stock value is low, the shareholders get paid in dividends. It is entirely your decision about what you want to do with that income. You could either invest it or keep it.

You get a lot of flexibility when it comes to trading stocks. Since millions of stocks are traded every day, you can easily sell shares and stocks or buy them whenever you want. This flexibility allows you to decide which company you want to invest in and when.

Another advantage of trading stock is that you own a part of the business. Depending on the timeframe and risk tolerance, the benefits can be many.

Businesses and individuals aren't the only two entities that reap the benefits of the stock exchange. The government also uses the stock exchange as a source of raising funds. Many national or state governments need funds to develop estate or community projects from time to time. Instead of raising the taxes, they issue bonds in the stock market. These bonds are bought by the investors through which the government raises the amount of money it needs to launch projects. In the long run, it helps the economy, increases the cost of living, and creates jobs.

Even when economies of countries like the UK and US are not doing so well, they are still construed as economic powerhouses. It is due to the economic perceptions. When countries' stock markets are strong, and on the rise, they are considered to be emerging economies. Their stock markets attract different economic activities that are beneficial to the country's economy, such as foreign investments.

Emerging economies are attractive to both foreign and local investors. However, sometimes things don't go in the right direction. When stock markets of emerging economies lose value, economic turbulence is felt across the globe. On October 29, 1929, also known as Black Tuesday, the US stock market collapsed, and The Great Depression happened. It threw the whole world into an economic downturn, and the entire spiral lasted for almost a decade. Many economists believe that The Great Depression happened due to the Black Tuesday. Therefore, some people consider investing in the stock market a very risky business, much like gambling. You are never too sure when the market will collapse, and you'll lose everything you invested.

Strategies for Buying Your Very First Stock

Investing in stocks is the most common way beginners start their investment journey. It is as easy as opening an account through a brokerage firm and buying stocks. Here are a few easy steps for buying your very first stock.

How to Invest

There are many approaches to investing in stocks. All you need to do is choose the option that is right for your needs. If you are a beginner, you may be a perfect candidate for a robo-advisor. It is a service that provides low-cost investment management. All brokerage firms offer this service. You invest money according to your goals. Once you have a preference, you are ready to open an account.

Investing Account

People who are well-versed in investing in stocks usually use a brokerage firm. For beginners, it is easier to use robo-advisor to open an account.

Both brokers and robo-advisors allow opening accounts with very little funds. An online broker provides the quickest and most inexpensive path to purchasing stocks, other investments, and funds. With a brokerage account, you can also open a retirement account or a taxable brokerage account if you want to save money for retirement in a different account.

Before opening an account through a broker, you have to do an evaluation of the broker firm such as costs, investor research and tools, investment selection, and so on. If these factors work for you, it's all well and good. If not, then look for another firm that fits your needs.

Know the Different Types of Stocks

If you are heading down the DIY path, then there are two investment types to choose from.

Exchange-Traded Funds or Stock Mutual Funds

Mutual funds allow you to buy small pieces of various stocks in one transaction. EFTs and index funds are funds that track an index. S&P's (Standard & Poor) 500 fund replicates the index by purchasing listed companies' stocks. Investing in a fund means you own small pieces of the companies' stocks you bought. You can invest in more than one fund to diversify your portfolio and spread the risk. Stock mutual funds are sometimes referred to as equity mutual funds.

Individual Stocks

If you want to invest in a particular company, you can either buy one or more shares as a way to ease into stock trading. It is easy to create a diversified portfolio by buying many individual stocks. However, it takes a lot of investment.

An advantage of stock mutual funds is that it lessens the risk since they are inherently diverse. For people looking to invest their retirement savings, a portfolio with mutual funds is the best option. However, mutual funds barely see a meteoric rise compared to individual stocks. If you decide to make wise investments when it comes to individual stocks, you can quickly experience success. However, the odds of you getting rich quickly are slim unless you have been in the game for a long time.

Setting Up a Budget

Beginners are always wondering how much budget they should set before planning on buying the stocks. The budget you need to purchase individual stocks depends on the price of the shares. Share prices typically range from a couple of dollars to thousands of dollars. If you want to invest in mutual funds but don't have a big budget, extended traded fund is the perfect choice for you. Mutual funds start at a minimum rate of $1000. ETF or extended-traded funds work like stocks and can be purchased for a share price as low as $100.

If you want to invest through funds, you can do so in the stock funds. Most financial advisors suggest doing this to their clients. It is a great choice if you are in it for the long-term. A 30 something-year-old's retirement investments will have 80% of the portfolio in stock funds, 20% would be in bonds. Keep individual stocks to a minimum in your investment portfolio.

Long-Term Goals

Investing in stock may seem like an easy way to make money by getting returns. In most cases, you lose more than you make in the short-term. There are many intricate strategies used by veteran investors for getting returns. The best thing for you to do is be in it for the long term. After you have invested in stocks, the best course of action is to forget they exist. Don't look at them. Unless you are involved in day-trading, compulsively checking your stocks won't do much.

Managing Stock Portfolio

Worrying about the fluctuations won't do much for you and your portfolio's health. Still, there will be times when you will need to check your investments and stocks. If you buy the stocks and mutual funds over time, checking your portfolio a few times is a good idea to ensure your investment goals are on track.

If you are close to retiring, you may want to move your stock investments to fixed-income investments.

Secondly, if you find your portfolio is heavily weighted in a single industry or sector, try to diversify by buying stocks or funds in a different sector. You could go for international stocks to get a bit more exposure and diversify your portfolio even further.

Tips for Investing in a Stock Market

Get the Basics Out of the Way

Before investing, deal with the basics first, such as paying off debts and building an emergency fund. You don't want to sell low investment stocks to cover your living expenses; having an emergency fund is crucial because it prevents scenarios like this.

Know Your Timeline and Goals

Before making an investment, figure out why you want to invest because different investment goals require different strategies. For instance, who wants to save their capital and draw income from it may build a more conservative portfolio by purchasing bonds of focusing on companies with less risk.

In the same way, someone wanting to grow their wealth in the long-run or build retirement savings may invest in stocks with higher returns in the future.

Understand Your Risk Tolerance

Another important tip to consider when investing in a stock market is to know and understand your risk tolerance. Even if you are in it for the long-run and want to expand your portfolio over time, evaluating personal risk tolerance may lead you to make less risky decisions.

Due Diligence

Whether you want to buy stocks or invest in bonds, mutual funds, etc., it is crucial to due diligence. That means researching each and every investment you make.

Public companies share paperwork to the SEC (U.S Security and Exchange Commission) every year. The paperwork consists of a company's expenses, revenues, account balances, and so on. Read these documents before investing.

Diverse Portfolio

As mentioned earlier in the book, diversifying your portfolio is important to spread the risk. The basic strategy of diversification is to purchase stocks from different companies. However, there are certain advanced strategies used by experienced investors.

For instance, some people split their portfolio profile by buying stocks with:

Different Market Capitalization

Market capitalization is the total value of the company's stocks.

Large-Cap Companies

Large-cap businesses have low returns but, at the same time, lower volatility compared to small-cap ones. They are worth more.

Having a mixture of companies in your portfolio gets you exposed to high-reward and high-risk of small caps, all the while getting the added benefit of low volatility large-caps.

Other people diversify the portfolio by having various investment types. For example, 70% of the portfolio will consist of stocks, and the rest will be bonds. Bonds are usually steady, whereas stock prices can be subjected to volatility. A mix of bonds and stocks forms a strong portfolio that helps you benefit from strong markets and reduces your losses during a slump.

Another great way of diversifying is by investing in mutual funds. Mutual funds take money from many different investors and then using it to purchase securities. One mutual fund holds thousands of various stocks.

You can also buy shares in a single mutual fund instead of 10 or 20. Keeping track of different funds can be a bit tedious.

Don't Allow Emotions to get in the Way

Whether you plan on investing on your own, with a mutual fund or robo-advisor, pay attention to your investments, and it's vital you don't invest emotionally in a company.

It can be easy to have your emotions and sentiments attached to certain brands or companies. However, liking a company is not the best reason to invest in it. Your investment decisions should be based on research and sound strategy.

Avoiding Leverage

For beginners, it can be tempting to use leverage or borrow money to invest, especially if the budget is not too high. Many brokers make it easy for you to have access to leverage. However, it is important to note that leverage is incredibly dangerous.

Investing in the stock market is a gamble. In an instant, you could lose all of your investments, even if the stocks you bought belonged to a steady business. Investing is exciting and a great opportunity to increase your wealth in the long-run. However, you need to study the market and tread carefully. Researching and following all the guidelines and tips is a surefire way of being successful in your investments.

Simple Rules for Making a Successful Investment

You may be intimidated by investing, especially in the stock market. Don't worry! You are not alone. Many people feel scared of the prospect of investing and the possibility of losing it all in a split second, especially if they plan on investing in individual stocks. They fear losing their savings and hard-earned money. Some people have experienced great financial losses because of stock investing. They became too greedy and wanted to make a quick buck only to have them lose everything. The fact of the matter is that stock market is a casino, and all investors are gamblers trying their luck every single day. If you don't follow the rules, you are bound to go home empty-handed.

You don't necessarily have to be good with numbers to be a decent investor. It is not as hard as it is deemed to be. All you need is emotional stability and key principles you need to abide by. You need to understand the industries and sectors you want to invest in and do extensive research. Warren Buffet's famous quote states, "All there is to investing is picking good stocks at good times and staying with them as long as they remain good companies."

Here are simple rules to help you invest successfully and build your wealth in a sustainable and safe manner.

Acknowledge Market Volatility

Investors need to accept market volatility. It is the main feature of stock markets around the world. As mentioned before, investing in the stock market is like gambling. High risks lead to bigger wins. You get higher returns from stocks that go through a lot of ups and downs in the market, and their share prices keep changing.

The stock exchange market goes through more volatility than you may realize. There is almost a 10% slump more than once in the market every year, and you might experience a 20% decline in the market once every five years. Every decade, you may experience an alarming 30% decline. Company stock prices are even more unstable, declining more than 50% in rate any time.

If one is not ready to face the market's volatility, they will be enticed to sell their investments at the first sign of a big slump. Selling during a massive drop is the worst mistake any investor could make. You must have faith that the market will recover, making new highs.

Hands-Off

Given the gyrations of the market, investors may be tempted to tinker with the investments. They should keep their hands to themselves. A London-based asset manager firm insists that investors "Buy good companies. Don't overpay. Do nothing."

In other words, don't compulsively check the portfolio every day. If you genuinely want to build your wealth, set long-term goals, invest, and let the market do the rest. If you keep checking your portfolio and the activities in the stock market, you may be tempted to buy more or sell some of your stocks.

Stick it Out

You can't time the stock market. Your stocks will occasionally experience setbacks. This is where emotional detachment comes into play. Don't get emotionally attached and stick to your convictions. If your six-month-old strategy isn't working presently, wait it out. Big gains come to those who are patient.

Set the Alerts

Don't trade for the sake of trading. Don't change your convictions unless there is a huge change in some of the stock in your portfolio. Then, you must review it.

 Investors tend to make mistakes and then forget about them. The most important trick is to recognize the mistakes made earlier, note them down, and never repeat them. What you need to do as an investor is to set the alerts. If a stock price falls below 20% the price originally paid by you, it should trigger the alert you set. This way, you would be able to review the original investment done by you and modify it accordingly.

If the prices haven't declined, then it is a great time for you to add to your portfolio. However, if your initial plan wasn't to increase your portfolio by buying more shares, then forget about it and move on. Don't become greedy.

Follow the Winners

Most investors spend all their energy on finding the best stock in the market only to realize that great stock is the one they already own. Sometimes, stocks that win keep on winning. That's why it works as a reminder for people to have faith in the companies they invest in.

All in all, typically, it's not the stocks that prove to be losers in an investor's portfolio. It is usually the stocks they chose to sell way earlier. Beaten-down shares have the tendency to bounce back, even if they don't become the biggest winners to drive the performance of the portfolio.

Cut Your Losses

If you find yourself losing 20% on a certain stock, there is no need to chase it. It will have to rebound 25% for you to break-even. However, it is important to point out that short-term stock losses become bigger overtime.

If a 20% loss goes on to become a 50% loss, then the stock has to double for you to break-even. The odds of recovering from this type of loss are quite slim. Therefore, it is best you cut your losses. Also, holding on to loss-making stocks is not a good look for an investor. It is simply a trait of a stubborn investor.

Don't Borrow, Beg, or Steal

Warren Buffet expressed his concerns about investors who borrow or indulge in leverage. He stated, "I've seen more people fail because of liquor and leverage – leverage being borrowed money." He further expressed his disdain by saying, "You really don't need leverage in this world much.

If you're smart, you're going to make a lot of money without borrowing," He added, "I've never borrowed a significant amount of money in my life. Never. Never will. I've got no interest in it. It is crazy in my view to borrow money on securities."

If a great investor like Warren Buffet didn't have to borrow and still managed to become one of the richest men on Earth, you don't need to either. However, there are still some investors who can't help themselves. The greed takes over them, and all that comes to their mind is "invest, invest, invest." They incur hundreds of thousands of dollars in debt, and when they lose their investments due to market volatility, they are left with no choice but to dive into their savings. It is a vicious cycle that starts with small leverage and goes on to ruin your financial security and then your life. The stock market is already a very risky business, and then to borrow money can lead you in a life full of troubles. Many people have been subjected to mental health issues and suicide ideation because they couldn't pay back the debts they incurred when investing in the stock market.

Keep a Look out for Taxes and Fees

Most beginner investors ignore taxes and fees. They assume a 0.5% brokerage fees won't impact their returns. Furthermore, who even thinks about taxes when investing until it's time to file the ITR, right? WRONG!

Don't forget to take into account all the hidden fees and brokerage payments when trading, when you sell or buy stocks. Even if the stocks you are selling are at a loss, you still need to pay brokerage. Also, taxes can't be ignored unless you want the IRS to knock on your door. If you want to successfully build your wealth, keep this rule in mind.

Stay On the Course

Changes in our lives, such as personal situation, economic environment, or change is legislation, can make us alter our wealth-building plan. Even the greatly formulated wealth plans require regular adjustments. To stay on the track, review your investment plans and portfolio from time to time. If there is a major change in your life, tweak your financial strategy to avoid poor performance in investment, unnecessary taxation, and other missed opportunities.

You should have your investments reviewed professionally so that you get sound advice from someone who knows the ins and outs of the financial and stock markets.

Different Types of Investments

Investing is intimidating for a fair amount of people. There are way too many options so it can be hard to know which one is the best. There are a few basic investment options that most people pick. However, you should choose one that suits your needs and works for your portfolio.

Stocks

Many people invest in stocks. Stocks are also referred to as equity shares. When you buy stocks at the stock market, you become one of the owners of a company. People who invest in stocks earn income through dividends. It is a risky form of investment because you could lose money if the company fails. How much, how often, and whether or not you make money depends on the stocks, fluctuations in stock market, economic conditions and so on.

If you want to diversify your investment portfolio, mutual funds and stocks can be good options. Do a lot of research before investing in a company.

Bonds

Bonds are another type of investment that most people go for. It is a loan paid to an organization, federal agency, or government by an investor in exchange for interest payments over time. There are several types of bonds, such as corporate, agency, treasury, municipal bonds, etc.

People also invest in bond mutual funds. When you invest in bonds, you risk losing money, especially if you purchased individual bonds and plan on selling them before their maturity dates. The prices of a mutual bond are subject to change.

Bonds can be an important component in your investment portfolio. Whether you are new to investing or a veteran investor with bonds in your portfolio, it is a sound method of investment.

Certificates of Deposit and Other Bank Products

Bank and other unions offer an easy and a safe way of making investment by accumulating savings. Banks tend to provide their clients various tools to help them manage their money. Bank deposits are insured and offer liquidity. You can access your funds anytime for unexpected emergencies, day-to-day expenses or down payment. You can also transfer money from your savings account to another payee or an organization. However, you must remember that interests on savings accounts are much lower compared to returns from other type of investments.

Investment Funds

Investment funds are where several investors pool money in an investment. There are different types of funds with several differing features. Publicly offered funds include exchange-traded funds, mutual funds, unit investment trusts, and closed-end funds. These funds have to be registered with the U.S. Securities and Exchange commission under the category of investment companies. Private funds also known as hedge funds don't have to get registered.

Investing in funds is an excellent and most flexible method of investment because they offer a variety of investment styles and strategies. However, as with any other investment method, you risk losing your money. The returns depend on the performance of the funds.

It should be noted that hedge funds are not forced to register with the Security and Exchange Commission (SEC). Therefore, unlike mutual and other publicly offered funds, they are not subject to any regulations outlined by the SEC.

Annuities

Annuities are contracts between a person and an insurance company. It involves the company promising periodic payments to the person starting either immediately or in the future. A person buys single or multiple annuities called premiums. Some people use annuities as savings from retirement. Others use them as a steady stream of income. Some people do both, save some annuities for retirement, and use the rest for their day-to-day expenses.

If you have an annuity on a vehicle and your payments are delayed to be paid out in the future, it is called a deferred annuity. However, if you used your annuity as a source of income during retirement, it is referred to as an immediate annuity.

There are two primary annuities, variable and fixed. There is also a hybrid annuity called fixed-index or equity-index annuity. Variable annuities are securities. They come under the Financial Industry Regulatory Authority.

Annuities are considered by investors as retirement savings. Therefore, it helps to understand and research about them. They are marketed as investments that are tax-deferred.

However, they come with their own sets of expenses and fees, such as mortality, surrender charges, administrative fees, expense risk charges, and so on. Annuities can also commissions that can be as high as 7% or more.

Retirement Savings Account

Come to think of retirement savings aren't exactly your investments, but they are an important element of financial management. For savings, IRA or 401 (K) is an excellent choice. Other than tax benefits, there is a possibility of your savings accumulating overtime.

Once you retire, having a hefty savings account can be the difference between running short of money down the line and living comfortably. If you haven't started saving up, now is the time to do so. It doesn't matter whether you have many years or are close to retiring.

Commodity Future Agreements

Commodity future agreements are contracts to sell or buy a certain quantity of a particular commodity at a specific price and date. These commodities include oils, metals, grains, currencies, financial instruments, and animal products. Trading usually takes place at commodity exchange. It is regulated by the Commodity Futures Trading Commission or CFTC, which is a federal agency responsible for regulating commodity options, trading markets, and commodity futures. Anyone trading with the trading futures with the public or giving advice about trading should be registered with the National Futures Association (NFA), an independent regulator.

Insurance

Life insurance is part of everyone's financial plan. Life insurance comes with several policies such as whole life, universal life, and term life. There is also variable universal life insurance or variable life insurance. These are securities that have to be registered with the SEC. Variable universal life products and firms and people selling variable life come under the jurisdiction of FINRA.

Insurance is often bought, depending on the buyer's specific objectives. For instance, long-term care insurance helps you manage health care expenses as you get older. Financial insurance, on the other hand, bought by businesses and comes with a number of fees. Always do extensive research before buying any type of insuring.

Here are the most commonly bought insurances.

Whole Life

This type is your ordinary permanent life insurance. It covers your whole life and builds cash value that is a savings feature. Premium payments for life insurance remain the same.

Variable Life

Variable life insurance works like security that offers a minimum death benefit and fixed premiums. Its cash value is in a portfolio of securities. You can choose to invest in a combination of policy offers. However, they don't guarantee any returns, and the cash value tends to fluctuate.

Term Life Insurance

Term life insurance covers a limited and specified period, called a term. Premiums for most of the term life insurance policies go up as you get older or closer to the end of every renewal period. As the term ends, so does the insurance policy and its coverage.

Universal Life Insurance

This insurance type provides coverage for life, and the premiums are flexible. The cost of protection and other fees are deducted from the policy or cash value.

Variable Universal Life Insurance

This type is the combination of variable life and universal life insurance. It provides the insured with flexible premium payments, coverage, and investment account.

Investing In Your Future: Retirement

Planning for your future involves saving up for retirement. To live a comfortable, secure, and happy life after retirement, you have to plant the seeds while you are young and still have a career. A financial cushion to soften the blow of retiring from a job with no steady income is crucial.

Start planning for your retirement by evaluating your retirement goals and the time it will take to achieve them. Then, you must start by researching on the type of accounts that will help you save for retirement and grow your wealth. Lastly, you have to think about taxes. There are several ways you can invest in your future. Here is a compilation of all the steps necessary to make sure you have a fruitful retirement.

Note Down Your Expenses

Make a list of all your expenses in order of priority. Cut down the ones with the lowest priority. The money you planned on spending on those expenses, consider adding them to your retirement account. You must remember you will not have a steady income post-retirement. It is absolutely crucial for you to try and save up as much as you can now, so you don't have any regrets later on.

Your Assets

Start evaluating your assets. You may be unaware of the income they may bring that you could add to your retirement savings. If you want to make extra money, restore your cars and sell them or auction off the antiques. If you are a great artist, sell your paintings or finish that half-written novel and publish it.

A lot of hobbies can be a source of income if you want it o. There are hundreds and thousands of ways to make money. When push comes to shove, people get creative. So, why not use your creativity now and make some extra cash for the sake of your future.

Monitor Your Health

Keep a check on your health. Make sure you eat healthy and workout. If you get sick with age, you will accumulate medical bills that reduce your savings. Try to lead a healthy life now. Go to the physician for an annual check-up. Healthy living doesn't have to be difficult. There are many fitness exercises, and you can eat healthy foods with your family. Exercise every day for at least half an hour, cut down on fast food, sugar, and you are good to go. You have to take care of your health. Think about you and your family's future.

Make Wise Investments

To make sound financial decisions, you might need a professional's help. Hire a financial advisor or spend time researching how you can invest wisely. There are many online risk-assessment tools you can make use of. They will give you some suggestions on how to go about the whole process of investment. Also, don't side-line your retirement savings. When making a decision to invest, retirement savings should be the top priority.

Consider mutual funds, exchange-traded funds, stocks and bonds to invest in. Also, invest in real-estate, silver and gold. If you have taken the route of self-directed IRAs, it can give you some autonomy on where you invest. Don't forget to diversify when considering your investments. This might take you some time, but doing so will ensure you don't lose out on all your investments if there is a dip in the economy. It is also an excellent way of building your wealth.

Choose When to Retire

Choosing your retirement date is crucial because that will determine how you secure it. If you plan on retiring late, you'd be able to save more. You can also delay your social security up until the age of 70. This will give you a higher monthly benefit. However, if you do decide to retire early and feel like you haven't saved enough, take up a part-time job. That way, you won't have to use your retirement savings for your day-to-day expenses. Part-time income will provide you with a steady source of income.

Having more money in your savings account will ensure a reasonable rate of return and add to your savings. You can take withdraw money from your savings without a penalty after the age of 59. This means if you wait a bit longer for retirement, you will be exempted from paying extra fees.

As mentioned earlier, you can work part-time. It gives those who have retired peace of mind, occupies their day and gives them more time to spend with their loved ones, all the while earning some money.

Create an Investment Plan

Formulating an investment plan may sound like a complex process, but it is very simple. All you need to do is evaluate your goals and risk-tolerance via a few crucial steps.

Step #1

The first thing you need to do is set your goals. List them down and categorize them into long-term and short-term goals. You must ensure they are practical and achievable.

Step #2

Starting earlier will serve you well in the long-run. To get good grades, you have to study way before your exam date; preparing to get the money to invest works the same way. The sooner you invest, the more wealth you'd be able to accumulate in the years to come. Waiting a long time to invest is going to make reaching your goals difficult.

Step#3

Consider time constraints and evaluate how they affect your risk tolerance. Time is of the essence when it comes to investment. If you invest earlier, you'd be able to afford a lot more risk. You will have time to experience the economic slump and then recover from it. Usually, people make money after the economy recovers. Also, starting early gives you a chance to be more aggressive and risky with your investments. Initially, you are allowed to be adventurous but as you reach closer to your goals, shift your investments towards more conservative strategies to protect them against a loss.

Step#4

Depending on when you need the money, you will decide where you should invest. For example:

If you need money in less than three years' time, you should consider investing in market funds or bond funds and short-term funds. Avoid investing in stocks as they are too volatile.

If you can afford five years before needing money, invest in stocks, but to diversify your portfolio and have a stable investment, invest in bonds and other cash equivalents. Since you don't have enough time to benefit from the market slump and the subsequent recovery, it is better to stick to more conservative investment strategies.

If you have anywhere from six to ten years or even more, you can invest in more stocks. In this case, it is more beneficial to invest in stocks rather than stable investments such as bonds. You will have enough time to see the economic slump and then reap the benefits when it shoots up, giving you handsome returns and enough money to invest in other strategies.

Step#5

When some people make investments, their focus is on the returns they will get. They don't think about the amount of money they could lose. In other words, they don't consider the risk of their investments. It is deeply important to assess your risk capacity when drawing out an investment plan. The mechanics of a market is that they tend to dip and then come up. Virtually every investment has some form of risk attached to it. Therefore, it is vital for new investors to understand the risk and then invest accordingly. Extensive knowledge about investment strategies and experience will help you understand whether you should invest aggressively, moderately or conservatively.

Step#6

Avoid putting all your eggs in one basket, meaning don't invest all your money in one strategy. Spread the risk by diversifying your portfolio. Invest in different sectors of the market and try not to chase the performance of your investments. When you have different types of investments in a portfolio, you avoid making mistakes by not moving your investments. Let your investments ferment.

Step#7

While it is impossible to control the markets you are investing in, you can minimize the taxes and costs. When it comes to investment, it is not only how much money you are making but also how much you are keeping. If you allow fees and penalties to constantly get deducted from investment capital, you won't have much left. Try to invest in strategies with low costs and always take advantage of tax-savvy strategies such as retirement accounts.

Step#8

Make an investment policy statement. It will help you guide the investment decisions. If you have a financial advisor, the investment policy statement will help you decide how to make your portfolio and where to invest.

Once you have a good plan in place, monitor your investments and balance your portfolio from time to time.

Ways to Avoid Risk

Risk is part of the investment, but there are some ways you can avoid it or mitigate it.

Be Diligent

It is vital to carry out extensive research before investing anywhere. For instance, if you want to invest in a stock, check the growth rate, debt load, PE ratio and then compare that information with other stocks in the same market sector. Stocks with unstable management, high PE ratios, inconsistent profitability, and low revenue growth can be ruled out.

Allocation of Capital

Divide your capital for investment between different classes of investments such as equity, debt or a bit of both. If a person starts investing earlier, then equity investment would be a smart choice. Equities offer higher returns, and any risk of inflation and volatility would be mitigated.

Diversification of Portfolio

This consists of investing in various products. For instance, if you plan on investing in equities, then do so in different sectors. This strategy typically gives lower returns.

However, the risk is substantially alleviated and protects against capital loss.

Monitor Your Portfolio

This goes without saying. You should keep a check on your portfolio at periodic intervals. For example, when the interest rates are low, the debt securities prices go up. It could be a chance for you to make some changes in your portfolio that could help you build more wealth in the future. However, if it is difficult for you to keep a regular check on your investment portfolio, then move to mutual funds. It will keep your investments safe.

Even when you invest in mutual funds, you have to evaluate the risk associated with the currency. Strong currency improves investment prospective, and weaker currency provides opportunities to invest in pharma companies and so on.

Investing in Blue-chip Company Stocks

To avoid risk, it is better to invest in frontrunner stocks or funds. However, you should keep an eye out for credit rating debt securities. Invest in better credit-rated securities to avoid risk.

The mechanics of investing money, return, growth, investment period, fees associated with it, and the risk tolerance have an impact on our goals. All types of investments carry some risk. What you do to minimize the risk is what determines how much wealth you are going to build. When investing somewhere, make sure you don't end up making up investment decisions that jeopardize your life.

Socially Responsible Investment

Socially responsible investment (SRI) means when you invest in companies that adhere to the ethical guidelines. The definition of SRI is broad because ethical standards vary based on who is evaluating them. A simple example of a company conforming to the social and ethical standards is one that uses green technology like solar panels to provide power to the factories making its products. You will be making a socially responsible investment if you decide to invest in the said company.

Another example of socially responsible investment is avoiding investing in companies that harm the environment or people, such as tobacco companies. While investing in a company that works on creating climate change awareness and tries to reduce its carbon footprint.

Socially responsible investment is carried out by people who have a connection to companies they want to invest in, or they want to invest in noble causes.

Different Types of Socially Responsible Investment Funds

There are different types of SRI investment funds. The traditional types of SRIs avoid companies that play a significant role in controversial activities such as alcohol, oil, firearms, tobacco and gambling.

The ERG Funds

Environment, social, and governance funds, also referred to as ERG funds, focus on excluding companies that don't use ethical products or practices. These funds specifically concentrate on companies that do uphold their ethical practices.

Impact Funds

These funds are ERG funds, but they focus on fund performance, unlike the ERG funds. It means that the company works on creating ethical changes with the services and products. Impact funds are great options if you want to be socially responsible but still want your stocks to perform. You must remember, though, the niche investments will provide you with fewer options to invest in.

Faith-Based Funds

These types of funds are not precisely socially responsible investments, but people only invest in stocks that abide by the rules of their religion, for instance, Catholic, Islamic or other Christian values. Any company that doesn't fit the category will be eliminated from the fund.

Benefits of Socially Responsible Investments

Socially responsible investments enable you to put your money where your mouth is. That means that if you say you want to be socially responsible, you prove it by investing in such companies. It is not easy being committed to changing the environment for the better, but you can only do your part. Investing in industries and companies that make an active effort to better our world is the best way to go forward.

When you invest in socially responsible investment, you are withholding your hard-earned money from going to industries that exploit the environment and the people. If more people leaned towards socially responsible investment, it would make harmful industries to do better and make ethical decisions.

By opting for socially responsible investment, assuming you are fully committed, you are able to sleep better at night knowing you have done everything in your power to do good. Although no human being is perfect, most of us want to make our world a better place to live in. If you can make a profit by being socially responsible, it is a win-win situation for all parties involved.

Perks of Attending Investment School for Beginners

A lot of people, after graduating from school or a university, start a job. That is a great choice, but if you want to build your wealth and or work in a sector that gives you more investment opportunities, attending an investment or a trade school might be a better choice.

There are several positive ramifications of going to a trade school. The skills and networking helping you move up on the career ladder and put your financial success on a fast track.

Here are some perks of attending an investment school:

Mentorship

The best part about going to a trade school knows that you will have a mentor with extensive knowledge about the market. None of the well-structured or well-written books can give you the unique knowledge that a mentor has under their sleeves. If you choose to take up an online trading course, well, it can only cover a few basics of the course. When you are exposed to a different scenario related to investments, your money is on the line. Instead of gambling, you could simply consult with your mentor. A mentor makes sure your investment practices start off on the right foot. If you make emotional investments in the initial stages of investments, your bad investment habits will be hard to break later on. Your mentor will make sure you don't make those mistakes. Through their experience, they would be able to guide you in the right direction.

Getting the Gist of What You are Doing

Trading is not like a high school test. You can't wing it. To fully understand what you are doing, you need to learn all the probabilities, structure, rules and information related to investment. When you study about certain factors affecting the performance of a company, that knowledge in itself is not enough. You need to understand why those factors affect the performance and how you can benefit from it.

In a trading and investment school, you will learn not to completely rely on pre-made trading blueprints. As informative as they may be, you are required to keep an eye out on the market.

Another perk of going to an investment school is the hands-on learning you will receive. Sitting in class and learning about the market isn't sufficient. Therefore, trading schools offer different tools and allow students to trade via simulated trading systems. They also give students access to the global markets using professional software used by traders.

Blaze a Trail

A beginner would be confused by all the information out there. There are certain investors and traders who claim they have found a "foolproof" method of making a lot of money. Not only is it statistically improbably, but it hurts a lot of newcomers as they fall into this trap. This is done to appeal to investors who don't want to learn about the market and want to invest, thinking they will be rich in a matter of weeks. That is not how the market works, and that is the reason most of the investors lose out on their investments. Attending an investment school helps you steer clear of such methods. The school encourages students to be trailblazers and form their own investment strategies that work with their goals. While risk-taking is part of trading, going all-in without prior knowledge is bound to get you into trouble. As you study and practice in school, you get more confident and slowly learn to take risks.

Resources

Besides learning the course, when you attend investment school, you are provided with additional resources that help you in the long-run. Since trading is a lifelong skill, investment resources can help you answer all your questions. You never stop learning when it comes to investment and stock markets. The resources provided include a lifelong membership program in which you can learn the course again if you want to. There are also other tools to help you get better at Forex trading, stock market investment and other commodities and options.

Conclusion

If you want to climb to the top of your career ladder, high school and university graduation aren't enough. If you want to be at a managerial position, then you need to have a few formal certifications under your belt. Employers looking for candidates for managerial positions want someone who has something that makes them stand out. Your education and experience at an investment school will qualify you for a larger salary package and a better position at a job. You will be exposed to many opportunities making enabling you to reach your goals. Learning about everything there is to know about investments, stock markets and then getting a formal education only adds to your list of accomplishments.

Disclaimer

Copyright © Year 2021

All Rights Reserved.

No part of this eBook can be transmitted or reproduced in any form, including print, electronic, photocopying, scanning, mechanical, or recording without prior written permission from the author.

This e-book has been written for information purposes only. Every effort has been made to make this eBook as complete and accurate as possible. However, there may be mistakes in typography or content.

The purpose of this eBook is to **encourage** people to invest in their lives and do things during their life that they can rejoice going back to their old age. The author and the publisher do not warrant that the information contained in this e-book is fully complete and shall not be responsible for any errors or omissions. The author and publisher shall have neither liability nor responsibility to any person or entity with respect to any loss or damage caused or alleged to be caused directly or indirectly by this e-book.